AF432700

QUERY CABOODLE 2
BY
HELLER LEVINSON
ARTWORKS BY
MOHSEN EL BELASY
AND
GHADAH KAMAL

Contents

SULPUR
EDITIONS

Query Caboodle 2

volts the psyche awake by tossing everything up for grabs. Nothing is certain. Nothing is presumed. By stripping away our smug conventions, Heller activates what is most human in us. Through the cleansing powers of unrelenting investigation, the sham & superficial dissolve, the lies & deceptions emaciate. We become *free* to approach the Miraculous, the Authentically Vital. This is a different approach to being-in-the-world, one which will make the everyday dazzle, the unrecognized glisten. As the poet Heath Brougher puts it: "This book made me realize that there were entire realms of ideas that I didn't even know I was supposed to be thinking about."

MOHSEN EL BELASY

where in

achieve

is

risk

how much of

prosperity

whence?

how much of

rapture

is

jurisprudence

why does talking to trees make so much sense?

MOHSEN EL BELASY

does mental illness occur in animals?

How

can we

verify?

what lays

beyond limits?

where in

mathematics

is

meander

Q. Is there mathematics without numbers?

What does it look like?

A. Yes, there is mathematics without numbers. In fact, some of the most fundamental branches of mathematics, such as topology and abstract algebra, do not rely on numbers at all.

Topology is the study of shapes and spaces, without reference to their exact size or shape. For example, a topological space is a set of points with a certain set of rules for how points can be connected to each other. These rules can be described without using numbers, and they can be used to prove theorems about shapes and spaces.

Abstract algebra is the study of abstract objects, such as groups and rings. These objects can be described without using numbers, and they can be used to prove theorems about other abstract objects.

There are many other branches of mathematics that do not use numbers. For example, graph theory is the study of networks, and it can be used to model real-world phenomena such as the spread of diseases or the flow of traffic. Game theory is the study of games, and it can be used to analyze strategic situations in business and politics.

Mathematics is a vast and ever-evolving field, and there is always more to learn. Even if you are not interested in the branches of mathematics that do not use numbers, there is no doubt that you will encounter them at some point in your life.

-- Chatbot

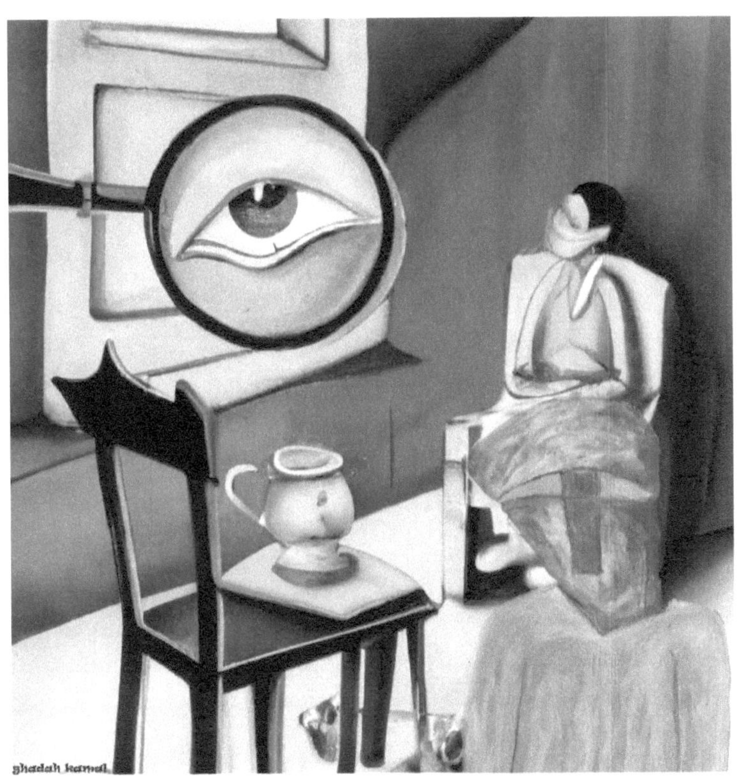
ghadah kamel

how much does the

drive for

recognition direct

one's life?

without recognition

does drive dissolve

is maintaining

drive without

recognition heroic?

why?

how much of

temperance

is

indecision

how much of

iridescence

is **travail**

Parmenides:

"You say there *is* the void; therefore the void is not nothing; therefore it is not the void."

how much of

void

is

hearsay

how many ships can water remember?

how much of

the seen

is

obscene

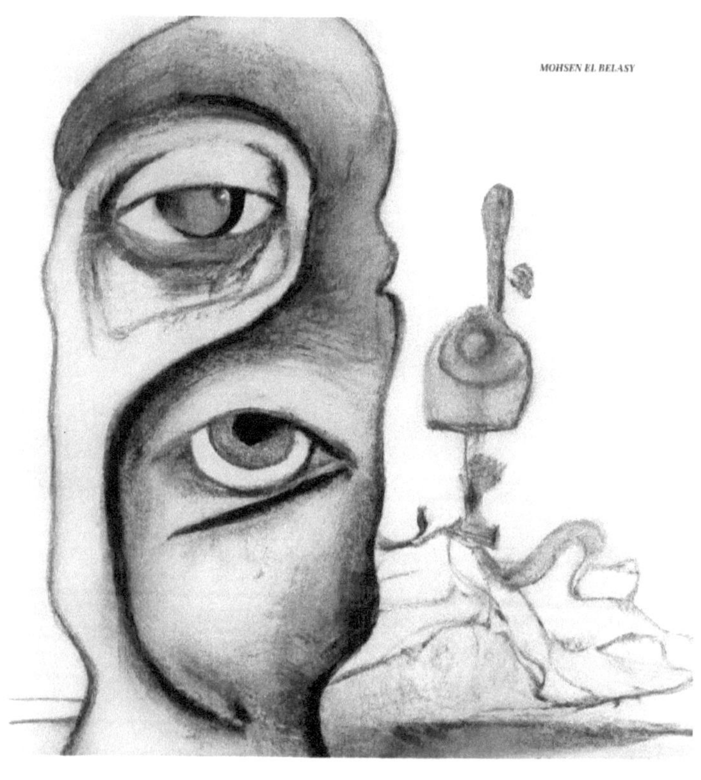
MOHSEN EL BELASY

how much of

sustainability is

porous

where

in the fallacy

is

redemption

where in the

blizzard

is

obscurity

how much of

wisdom

is

unsuspecting

how much of

wisdom

is

unmitigated

ghadah kamal

how much of

wisdom

is

unmistakable

how much of

wisdom

is

incalculable

why so often in a

relationship is the

question asked:

Where is this

headed?

Is love geographic?

Does it possess

a cardinal

direction? North?

East? South? West?

North by

northwest?

Would the correct

response to the

question be to pull

out a compass?

where in the

dissolution

is

bustle

where in the

bustle

is

bristle

why do humans
gobble up new
technologies like so
much cotton candy?
what's the fierce

attraction?

where in the

approach

is concern

ghadah kamal

how

much of

love

is

anchorage

how much of

love

is

accidental

where in the

accidental

is

outcome

where in the

quickening
is

apparatus

how

much of

apparatus

is

immaterial

do relationships

have a critical mass?

how many kinds of
infinity are there?

MOHSEN EL BELASY

how many kinds of
insanity are there?

how much of

perplexity is

inattention

how much of

intelligence

is

artificial

where in the

dislodge

is

conviction

how does

conviction relate to

integrity?

is dislodgement

integral to

revelation?

is integrity the

same as truth?

does truth have
integrity?

how much of

integrity

is

claustrophobic

It is posited that

one day

quantum

computers may

be able to

"find the meaning

of the universe."

Will it prove meaningful?

where in

dismissal

is

abundance

ghadah kamal

where is the color

that will change my

mind?

where in the lift is

loftiness

how much of

diffidence

is

deferral

how much of

wherewithal

is

capacity?

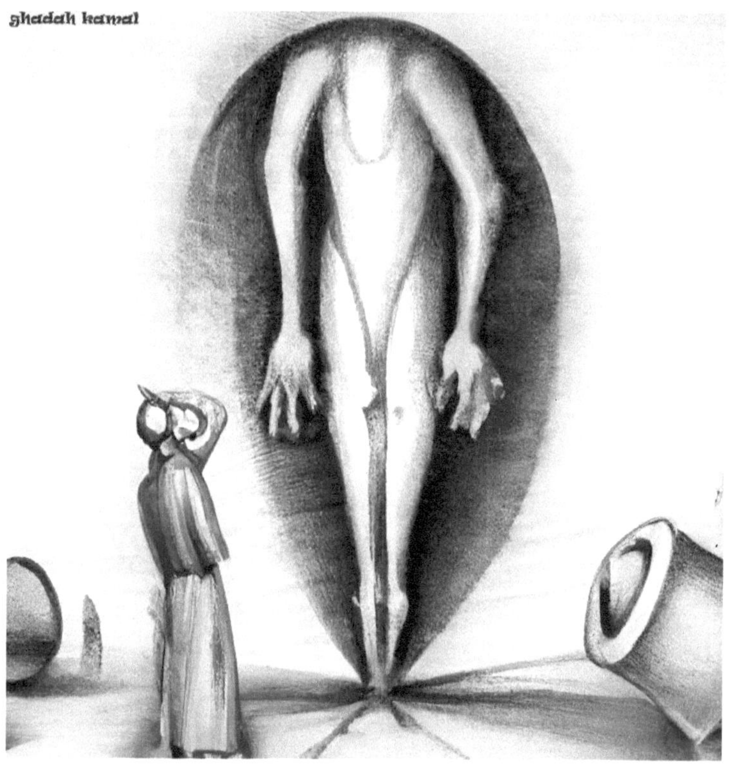
ghadah kamal

how much of

perplexity

is

maladjustment

how much of

perplexity

is

fact finding

how much of

enterprise

is

jurisdiction

where in

the

constitution

is

remorse?

MOHSEN ELBELASY

sully?
redemption?

why are

slights so

painful?

how

much of

gloom

is

disrespect

how

much of

infidelity

is

indifference

where in

procedure

is

recompense

ghadah kamal

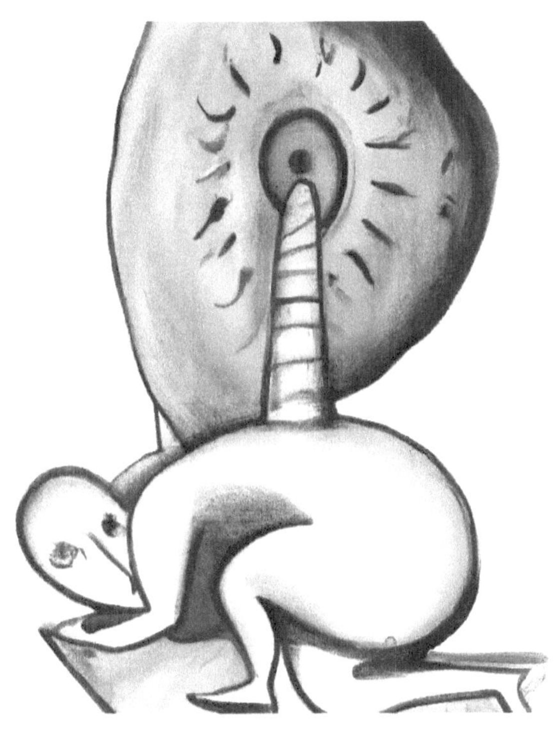

where in

surreption

is

outbreak

how much of

perception is

procreative?

if

a perception is not

procreative is it

perceptive?

does

madness

have a short

form?

how much of

indifference

is

surmountable

how much of

order

is

subterfuge

MOHSEN EL BELASY

is true love true if it
vanishes?

where in the

abyss

is

rectitude

how

much of

love

is

non-resistance

how

much of

translucence

is

romance

Can the Abyss sport a Beyond?

how much

of the abyss

is voidable

can

the voidable

be a-*voided*

how much of

voidable is

anfractuous

where

in anfractuosity is

blend

how much does the

proposition glow

how

much of

austerity

is

replacement

how much of

intimacy is

activation

how much of

perilous is

overlooked

how much of

architecture

is

discussions

The 'discussion' this query seeks to explore are the non-human inter(weavings)courses between angles, planes, windows, lighting, shadows, glass, mortar, wood, chimney, chair, table, spaces,etc.

MOHSEN EL BRASY

how much of

temporality

is

suburban

how much of

intimacy

is

ambidextrous

how much of

hysteria

is

non-contingent

can love

be learned

how much of

history

is

ambidextrous.

how much of

wary

is

self-annihilative

when the sex goes

how
much

love

remains

MOHSEN EL BELASY

how much of

eerie

is

unsurprising

how

much of

intimacy

is

organization

are you unanimous?

u u u u   you

u

nanimous

parse

dwindle

darn

drive

are you unanimous

{thistle
plump blossom
berry

{adorn unadorn
forlorn

u u u u

retrospect

divine

↓

unanimous

sublime

u   u

u

reckless deckless

uninform uniform

unanimously you

pitstop

furlough

farfalle

Pittsburgh

how many ways to

clinch a thing

ditch a thing

cinch a thing

stitch sew pinch

pleat cleat rub your

feet

ring-a-ding

ringring

anybody home?

how do you do?

fine day

ARE YOU

UNANIMOUS

UNANIMOUS

UNANIMOUS

where in the

limit

is

exaggeration

how much of

through

is

thorough

where in the

sadness

is

homecoming

where in the

windfall is

perforation

where in the
forgetting

is

cornucopia

MOHSEN EL BELLSY

If, according to
Heidegger,
Dwelling is the
becoming homely
of a being
unhomely,
how much of
dwelling
is
making

where in

latency

is

tribal reflex

where in the release

is

abandon

ghadah kamal

why is it so difficult
to remain in love?

where in the

ecumenical

is

porous

how much of

illumination

is dismissal

how

much of

dismissal is

a cover-up

ghadah kamal

how much of

love

is

extermination

where in

the

abysmal

is

abscess

how can the word

avoid becoming

a compartment?

how does naming challenge intimacy?

ghadah kamal

how does naming

enhance intimacy?

when a child points
& asks
'what's that' & a

name is proffered,

does the inquiry

stop

where in

the

poem

is

wound

reacting to the

phrase in a friend's

poem that reads:

'poem as wound'
I email: This opens

up all sorts of stuff.

Can the poem itself

be the wound?

by scapeling into

the human psyche

are we opening up

horrors? demonic

matters?

or the wound as the

human condition

(the human as a

product of

evolutionary

overkill),

& the poem

sloshing about in

the verminous

infection.

&/or, is the poem

the antidote to the

wound? an exercise

in stitching/healing

the trauma?

&/or could the

poem be a wound

facilitator,

galvanizing a

contiguous *wound*

reaction?

wound ://: poem

://: = the see-saw

symbol further

explained in *from

stone this running*

(BWP, 2011).

Yours in the Quest,

Heller

where in the

perpendicular

is

paradox

how much of

love

is

ambidextrous

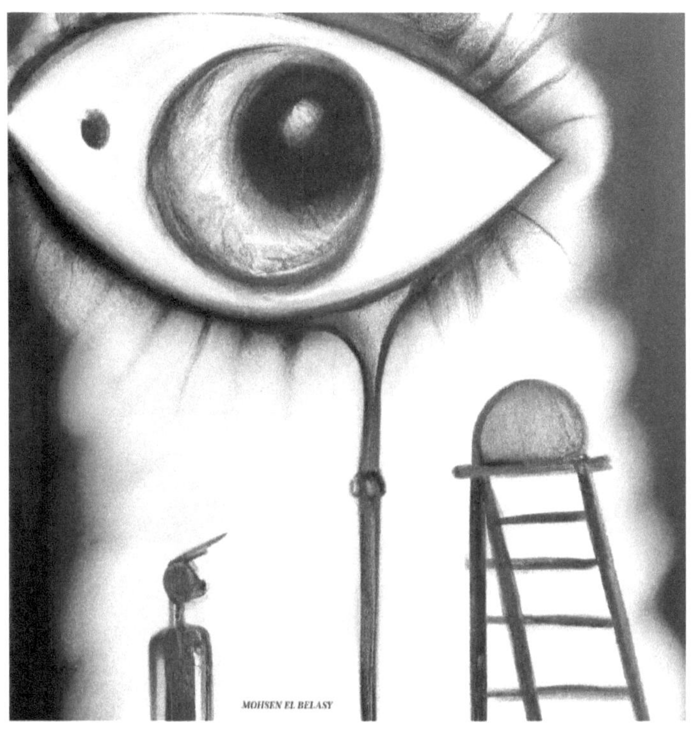
MOHSEN EL BELASY

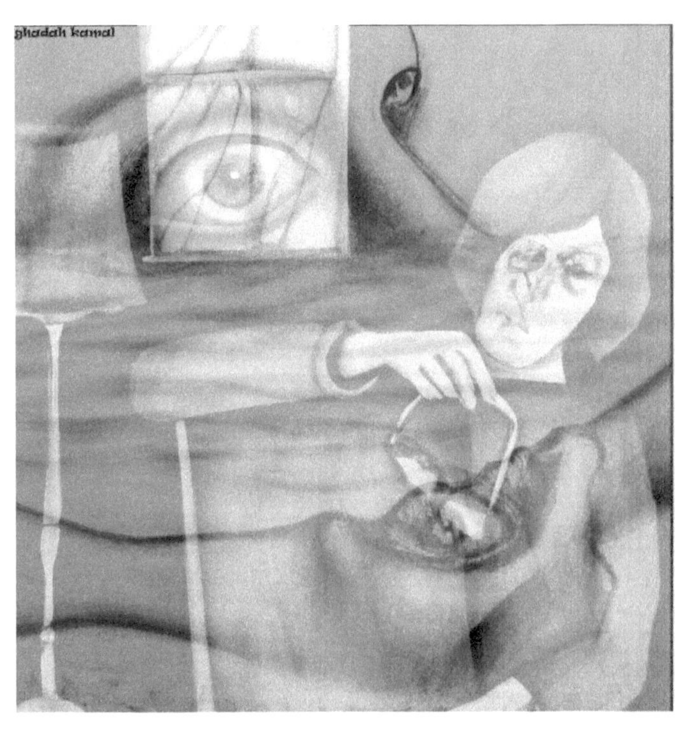
ghadah kamal

LA BELLE
INUTILE
EDITIONS

www.ingramcontent.com/pod-product-compliance
Lightning Source LLC
Chambersburg PA
CBHW051444130726
47987CB00005B/2177